Let's Look at Emergency Vehicles

John Allan

HUNGRY TOMATO™

MINNEAPOLIS

Thanks to the creative team:
Editor: Tim Harris
Design: Perfect Bound Ltd

Hungry Tomato®
A division of Lerner Publishing Group, Inc.
241 First Avenue North
Minneapolis, MN 55401 USA

For reading levels and more information,
look up this title at www.lernerbooks.com.

Main body text set in Fibra One Alt.

Library of Congress Cataloging-in-Publication Data

Names: Allan, John, 1961– author.
Title: Let's look at emergency vehicles / John Allan.
Other titles: Emergency vehicles
Description: Minneapolis, MN : Hungry Tomato, a
division of Lerner Publishing Group, Inc., [2019] |
Series: Mini mechanic | Audience: Ages 6–9. | Audience:
Grades K to 3.
Identifiers: LCCN 2018049645 (print) | LCCN
2018051361 (ebook) | ISBN 9781541555365 (eb pdf) | ISBN
9781541555358 (lb : alk. paper)
Subjects: LCSH: Emergency vehicles–Juvenile
literature. | Rescue work–Juvenile literature.
Classification: LCC TL235.8 (ebook) | LCC TL235.8 .A45
2019 (print) | DDC 629.225–dc23

LC record available at https://lccn.loc.gov/2018049645

Manufactured in the United States of America
1-45935-42829-1/10/2019

Contents

The Mini Mechanics

This is a claw hammer. One end is used to pull nails out and the other to hit hard objects.

Rescuers may use an angle grinder to open jammed car doors.

We are the mini mechanics. Welcome to our workshop. We work on some amazing emergency vehicles, and here are a few of the tools we and the rescuers use.

We will need a large wrench for undoing large bolts.

All rescue vehicles carry fire extinguishers to put out fires.

Ambulance

Ambulances carry sick or injured people to the hospital in emergencies. Ambulances have a lot of equipment to keep people alive.

Ambulances have loud sirens and flashing lights to tell other people to get out the way when they are driving to an emergency.

Ambulances have highly trained paramedics to look after sick and injured people.

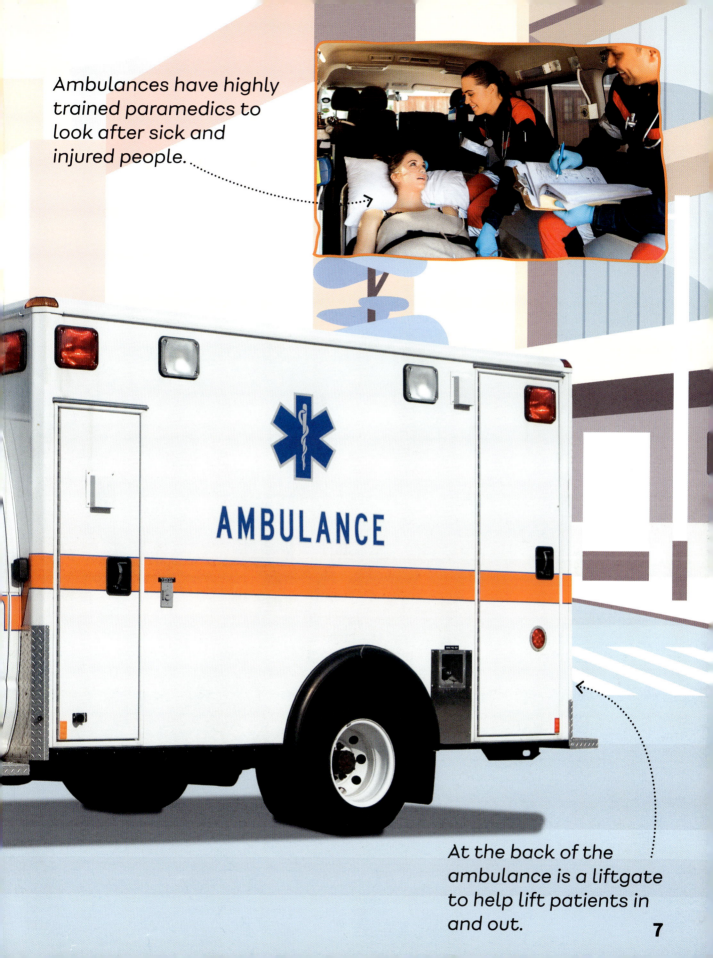

At the back of the ambulance is a liftgate to help lift patients in and out.

AMBULANCE

Fire Truck

These fire trucks rush firefighters to the fire. They have all the equipment they need to fight fires and rescue people.

This fire truck is putting out a fire on the side of the road.

Water is sprayed on fires through hoses. When they are not being used, the hoses are folded flat and stored here.

Hoses attach to the water tank here.

Search & Rescue Helicopter

This is the MH-65 dolphin, a search and rescue helicopter. It has two pilots, a flight mechanic, and a rescue swimmer.

These rotor blades lift the helicopter into the air. It can fly up to 200 miles (320 km) per hour.

A rescue swimmer is jumping out of the helicopter to rescue someone in the water.

6551

NORTH BEND

DANGER

KEEP AWAY

BEWARE OF BLAST

OAST GUARD

EXHAUST

65D

This small rotor is used to steer the helicopter when it is flying.

Fireboat

Fireboats are used to fight fires on ships and buildings that are close to the water. They have large pumps to spray water onto the fires.

Fireboats sometimes shoot water in the air to welcome naval ships.

This nozzle shoots water at a fire. It can spray water as far as 400 feet (120 m).

The captain of the ship controls it from a room called the bridge.

Police Car

Police cars are used for patrolling or responding to crimes. They have distinct colors so people can identify them. Police cars can chase criminals at high speed.

Police cars can drive over 130 miles (200 km) per hour.

This police officer is using an in-car computer. It can be used for contacting the police station.

This car has extra strong sides to protect the officers inside.

Airport Crash Tender

An airport crash tender is a special truck for fighting fires at airports. They are usually very big.

They have big wheels so that they can drive over wreckage.

Crash tenders have powerful nozzles to spray foam on burning planes. The foam puts out the fire.

They carry lots of foam in tanks.

Rescue Submersible

This is a rescue submersible. It saves sailors from submarines that are in trouble. It is carried to the rescue site by a mother ship.

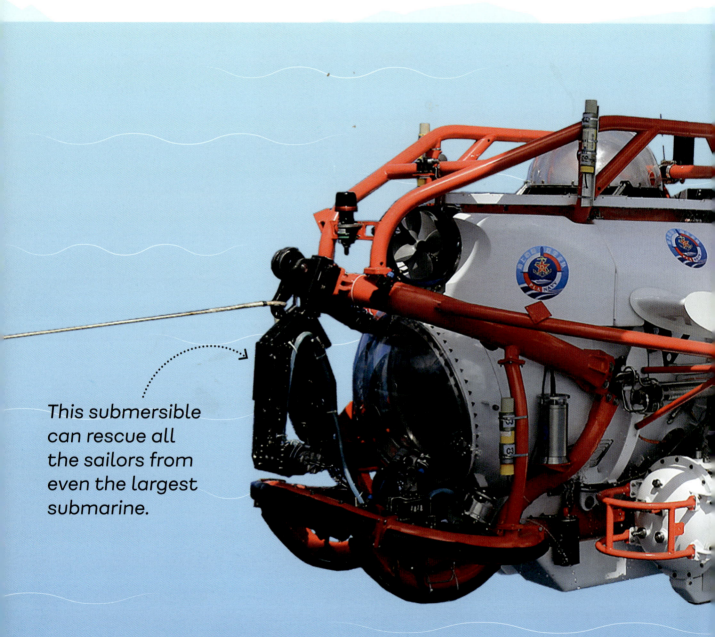

This submersible can rescue all the sailors from even the largest submarine.

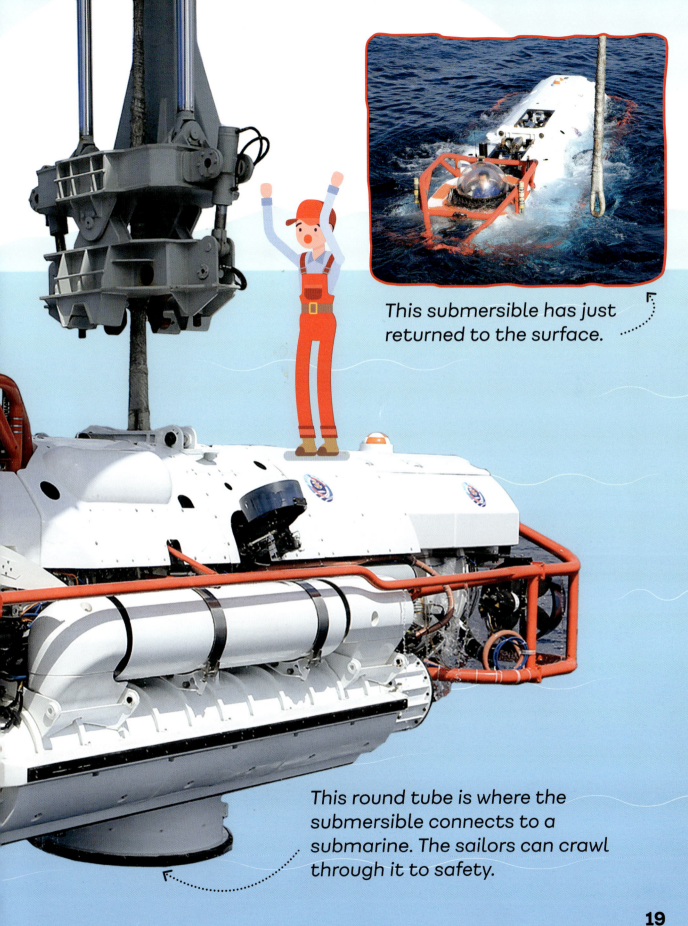

This submersible has just returned to the surface.

This round tube is where the submersible connects to a submarine. The sailors can crawl through it to safety.

Snowblower

When roads are blocked by snow, a snowblower will clear them. It collects the snow and blows it onto the side of the road.

Snow is sprayed up this chute and away from the road.

As the truck moves along, it clears a path through the snow.

Blades on a drum at the front churn up the snow. As the drum spins, it flings the snow out of the chute.

Chains stop the wheels from slipping on the snow.

Lifeboat

This is a lifeboat to rescue people at sea. It is designed to sail in all weather. It can completely roll over and still sail on.

This lifeboat is on patrol on the Potomac River in the US.

This door will not let water in, even if the lifeboat is upside down.

When the weather is bad, the crew stays inside and controls the ship from here.

Glossary

bridge: a room from where a boat is driven

churn: stir violently

mother ship: a ship that sends out smaller craft

nozzle: a device that directs and speeds up the flow of a liquid

patroling: driving around an area, looking out for criminals

rotor: the spinning part of a helicopter or machine

tailgate: a gate at the rear of a vehicle that can be let down to form a flat surface

workshop: a place where things are made or repaired

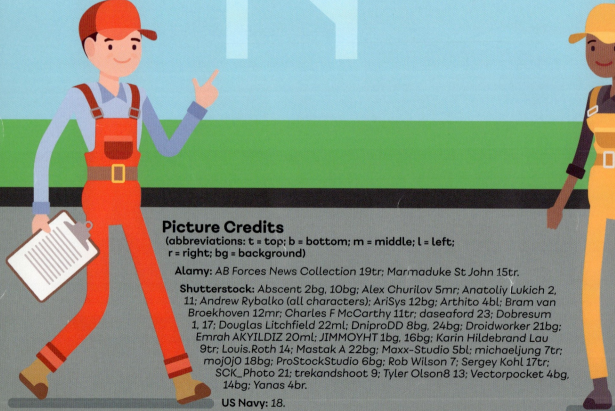